Special thanks to Judy Doran for her encouragement and support in creating this book.

Count on the USA!

Text and illustrations copyright © 2026 Kerrie Miller

Published by Red Cardinal Press

All rights reserved.
No part of this publication may be reproduced, distributed, or transmitted in any form or by any means, including photocopying, recording, or other electronic or mechanical methods, without the prior written permission of the publisher, except in the case of brief quotations embodied in reviews and certain other noncommercial uses permitted by copyright law.

The moral rights of the author and illustrator have been asserted.
Cover design and illustrations by Kerrie Miller
Board book ISBN: 979-8-9880590-1-1
Paperback ISBN: 979-8-9880590-2-8
Library of Congress Control Number: 2025926913

NO AI TRAINING: Without limiting the author's [and publisher's] exclusive rights under copyright, any use of this publication to "train" generative artificial intelligence (AI) technologies to generate text or pictures is expressly prohibited. The author reserves all rights to license this work for generative AI training and development of machine learning models.

Count on the USA!

Written and Illustrated by: Kerrie Miller

For all the brave men and women who protect our country, and for the families who love and support them.

A portion of the profits from the sale of this book will be donated to

Friends of the Troops

friendsofthetroops.org

Uncle Sam is a popular symbol for the United States. He represents patriotism, duty, and unity. Uncle Sam is dressed in red, white, and blue to match the colors in the American flag.

1

one

The Statue of Liberty stands on Liberty Island in New York Harbor and represents freedom and hope.

2

two

The Liberty Bell is a symbol of freedom and independence and is displayed in Philadelphia. This bell is famous for its large crack.

3

three

The rose is the national flower of the United States. Roses are a symbol of love and beauty.

4

four

The American bison, the largest mammal in North America, is officially recognized as the national mammal of the United States.

5
five

The Mayflower was a ship that sailed from England to North America many years ago. The passengers were pilgrims who settled in Massachusetts after the long journey.

6
six

The bald eagle is the national bird of the United States and a powerful symbol of freedom and strength.

7

seven

The oak tree is the national tree of the United States. There are many species of oak trees, and they can be found throughout our country.

8
eight

The White House is located in our country's capital, Washington, D.C. This is where the president lives and works.

9
nine

The American flag is red, white, and blue and is a symbol of freedom. The American flag is often referred to as “Old Glory.”

10
ten

1
2
3
4
5

6 

7 

8 

10 

www.ingramcontent.com/pod-product-compliance
Lightning Source LLC
LaVergne TN
LVHW070208110826
845147LV00002B/537

* 9 7 9 8 9 8 8 0 5 9 0 2 8 *